THE BOUNCE BACK QUOTIENT

This Book is a Gift

From:

_____

To:

_____

THE BOUNCE BACK QUOTIENT

**52 Action Oriented Ideas
For Bouncing Back From Any
Change Or Setback In Life**

Linda Nash

Prism Publications
St. Louis, Missouri

The Bounce Back Quotient

52 Action Oriented Ideas for Bouncing Back
from Any Change or Setback in Life

Linda Nash

Copyright © 2000 Linda Nash

Published by:
Prism Publications
St. Louis, Missouri

All rights reserved.
No part of this book may be used or reproduced in any manner
whatsoever without written permission from the author.

Printed in the United States of America

ISBN: 0-9636702-2-0

Dedication

To all the people who have loved, supported and guided me through the years. And, to all the people who have hurt, devalued, betrayed my trust, and been unfair to me. All of you have taught me meaningful lessons about resilience. You have shaped who I am today.

Acknowledgments

My sincere thanks to all my clients, both individuals and companies. You helped me realize the great need for this assessment and book and provided the quantity and depth of information needed to make it accurate and valuable.

To my speaker group Karyn Buxman, Lois Creamer, Steve Epner, Tony Ruesing, Sam Silverstein, and Carol Weisman, thank you for your encouragement, advice, and support. My Bounce Back Quotient has improved because of you.

To my dear friends, Sam Silverstein, and Karen Butery for your invaluable editing and fearless critique. To Pam Vaccaro and Bill Browning who took the time to review the manuscript, to VIP Graphics for the cover photo, and to Jim Weems of Ad Graphics for his design work and patience. A special thanks to Chris Scavotto for the original BBQ design.

Table of Contents

Foreword 9

Introduction 11

Bounce Back Quotient Self Assessment 14

Assessment Scoring 18

Guide & Action Steps to Improve Your BBQ 22-125

New Beginnings 127

About the Author 129

Foreword

Had I done the Bounce Back Quotient™ self assessment 20 years ago, my score would have been in the basement. Oh, I'd survived many things, as most people have, but every bad choice and mistake of my life had me by the throat, internally. I was insecure, fearful, and angry. Although my facade was one of success and happiness, I was a fake. Many of us are. It took its toll on my energy, my ability to function, and my self esteem. Those closest to me also paid a price. I thank my survival instinct for pushing me to read, study, and eventually decide that I could create a different kind of life. A happy, fulfilled, truly successful, integrated life.

Developing true resilience meant major changes for me. I was more scared than ever before in my life. Fear is a mighty obstacle. I pressed forward anyway. Slowly, I emerged into a calmer place. The fear didn't vanish, but a new self assurance, a lightness, a joy I had never known began to spill into my days. The internal me began to match the external me.

This transformation is possible for anyone, however entrenched your perspective or habits. The 52 ideas in this book can guide you to a more resilient life.

I have worked with thousands of people in companies nationwide through reorganizations, downsizings, mergers and acquisitions. As I documented my work, patterns emerged. There was a commonality among the resilient. It wasn't age, race, culture, or gender. I began identifying the specific principles. With the gathered data and my observations, it was possible to accurately predict which companies and individuals would succeed and which ones would fall flat or take longer to recover.

Synthesizing my information with the work already done on resilience, much of it tracking abused children and those of alcoholic parents, I developed and tested the Bounce Back Quotient™. These easy to understand ideas have already guided many to happier, more productive, and satisfying lives. Assess your BBQ™ and begin increasing your bounce backability today.

Introduction

Why do some people, companies, and organizations bounce back and thrive no matter what happens? What is it that makes them so resilient that they can consistently excel while others are left running in place, or worse, slipping backwards? It's a high Bounce Back Quotient.™ The BBQ is a specific combination of characteristics, attitudes, beliefs, habits and the triggers that influence them.

Life is filled with tests. From spelling and math to loss and pain, we are repeatedly given the opportunity to prove our knowledge and ability to ourselves and the world. If we don't do well the first time, we get to take the test again. When we pass, we go to a higher testing level. If not, we may get stuck repeating the same level.

As with school, so with life. Bounce backability begins in childhood and develops throughout our lives. Every frustration, problem, or setback tests our ability to deal effectively with the pragmatic and emotional issues. With every success comes greater strength and with every problem comes a new opportunity to succeed.

We know that brains are wired differently. Activity in the prefrontal lobes can predict a positive or negative orientation. Some people are born more positive and less anxious. Rewiring is possible, though. Ultimately, your view of the world and how you adapt depends on experiences created by parents, teachers, random situations, and finally, you.

Each life challenge adds to or takes away from your Bounce Back Quotient. It's like adding to or subtracting from a bank account. The lower your account is, the less money you have to deal with debts. If your BBQ is low, you won't bounce back easily from setbacks.

Recall the changes in your work and life over the past five years. How have they impacted you? Your work? Your family? Whether it's ending a personal relationship, losing a job of 20 years, seeking your first job, corporate re-structuring, dealing with new technology, or the death of a loved one, each of us is required to face emotional setbacks and change. Whether you fall flat or bounce back is within your control.

What is in your BBQ account? This book will tell you. The ability to bounce back is more than surviving. It is being able to recover from any setback and move forward both internally and externally. It is thriving.

Some people appear resilient when internally they are holding onto past emotional issues such as hurt, anger, or fear. They're unhappy, at best. Eventually unhappiness is externalized in the form of extreme self-centeredness, aggressive behavior, poor performance, shattered relationships, subterfuge, or withdrawal. Resilience brings less stress, more productivity, greater innovation, and a more fulfilling life.

This book provides a clear guide to the principles for becoming more resilient. Use these steps to improve your specific areas of weakness and you'll bounce back faster, better and higher!

Begin by taking the Bounce Back Quotient self assessment and determining your score. Be honest with yourself. After you complete the assessment you can either go to the numbers where your score is low and determine what you need to do, or proceed through the entire book reviewing both your strengths and weaknesses. In either case, you will have a guide and action steps for improving your BBQ and increasing your bounce backability account. Step-by-step you can achieve the skill needed to get to the eye of any storm and create the future you desire.

Bounce Back Quotient™ Self Assessment

Mark the number that best indicates the extent to which each statement is true for you.

1	2	3	4	5
Little or none	Some extent	Moderate extent	Great extent	Very great extent

1. I use words like choice, can, and will rather than can't, try and maybe. ____

2. I look for ways to keep growing personally and professionally. ____

3. I see negative events as a temporary setback, which I can get through. ____

4. I believe it is my responsibility to continue my education or skill building. ____

5. I surround myself with people who support and encourage me. ____

6. When an unexpected change occurs, I view it as an opportunity to experience something new. ____

Subtotal for this page ____

7. I ask for advice or help when dealing with a difficult situation. ___

8. I am willing to take reasonable risks when I recognize a new opportunity. ___

9. When my life or work isn't going in the direction I want, I take responsibility and get busy making a plan for change. ___

10. I have confidence that I can learn to do almost anything if I work at it. ___

11. When dealing with a new way of doing things, I persist until I'm successful. ___

12. When I have a setback or failure, I look for the lesson and move on. ___

13. I congratulate myself for accomplishments and appreciate the work I've done. ___

14. I don't procrastinate when I have an important task to do. ___

15. I believe I have an inner or higher source of strength to call on when everything seems to be going wrong. ___

16. I watch less than two hours of TV daily. ___

17. I sleep or nap 10 hours or less within a 24 hour period. ___

18. I forgive myself and move on, when I feel I've made a wrong choice. ___

19. I let go of old friends or business acquaintances if they are no longer supportive. ___

Subtotal for this page ___

20. I look for new and better ways to accomplish tasks. ___
21. When I make a mistake, I take responsibility. ___
22. I weigh the consequences of my actions when I make a decision. ___
23. My work is compatible with my values. ___
24. While I think of others, I value and take care of my needs. ___
25. I always read the "handwriting on the wall" and decide what I need to do. ___
26. My actions match my words. ___
27. When bad things happen, I mourn the loss, understand that this is life and move on. ___
28. I am aware that everything I do is a choice, even not choosing. ___
29. I do my best even when I don't like a particular job. ___
30. I prioritize and break large tasks into manageable parts. ___
31. I believe that life is for living and enjoy it all. ___
32. When offered an opportunity for leadership, I'll accept and learn all I can. ___

Subtotal for this page ___

33.	I believe bad hair days, soggy sandwiches, or bad coffee are just a part of life, no big deal.	____
34.	When a problem arises, I face it and set about finding a solution.	____
35.	I have created a "safe space" or oasis where I feel comfortable and relaxed in life.	____
36.	I believe that I am in charge of my life.	____
37.	I always bounce back quickly from any change or difficulty.	____
38.	I have daily rituals, which provide a sense of stability even in chaotic times.	____
39.	I believe I have a purpose in life.	____
40.	I have a mentor who provides direction and support in my work and life.	____
41.	I am active in a professional or civic organization.	____
42.	I commit to a goal even if it requires sacrifice on my part.	____
43.	I delegate when someone else can handle a task.	____
44.	I feel positive about my life and future.	____
45.	I am flexible and adapt easily and quickly to changes and new situations.	____
46.	I collaborate effectively with other people.	____
47.	I accept my limitations, value my gifts, and keep growing.	____

Subtotal for this page ____

48. I keep putting one foot in front of the other when things are rough. ____

49. I recognize that growth for people and companies requires change. ____

50. I realize that new problems require new solutions and look for them. ____

51. I develop and maintain mutually beneficial relationships in my work and life. ____

52. My sense of humor and ability to laugh and have fun help me deal with problems. ____

                        Subtotal for this page ____

SCORING

        Write your Subtotals here page 14 ____

                                       page 15 ____

                                       page 16 ____

                                       page 17 ____

                                       page 18 ____

Add your Subtotals for your Total. Write it here. ____

Compare your total with the ranges below.

210-260   Congratulations! You'll bounce back quickly and easily, and get on with work and life. Review your weaker areas and improve them to insure that you will always bounce back faster and higher. To stay on track, review your BBQ™ each year.

159-209 You'll bounce back from most things, but it will take longer or you may get stuck in a few areas. Review your weak spots and work to raise your score a few points each week. Keep track of your improvement, congratulate yourself and keep moving forward.

108-158 Your bounce will be low and slow. You may pretend that everything is fine, but it will take you longer with considerable ups and downs before recovering from a difficult or frightening situation. Begin working immediately on your weakest areas. Take one each week and concentrate on raising your score. As you add each point, be proud of your success. You'll be bouncing higher and faster and moving to the next level.

52-107 You'll hear more of a thud than a bounce. You feel like a victim and get stuck in fear or anger when changes occur or difficult situations arise. Look at your weakest areas. Develop a plan for improvement, and stick with it. Try to raise your score just a few points each week. Track your improvement. You'll begin to notice the difference. So will the people around you. Reward yourself and know that your bounce backability is improving daily.

NOTE: If you scored under 3 on any of the statements, review them and make changes in your life, work, or attitude to increase those scores.

Copyright © 2000 Linda Nash
All rights reserved.

Congratulations! Whatever your score, you have taken the first step toward a more resilient future. If you scored in the top group, but don't feel happy with your life, review to be sure that you aren't deceiving yourself. If you scored in the bottom group, don't despair. This is an opportunity to change your life one step at a time.

Remember that your ability to bounce back is like a bank account. You add to it or subtract from it every day. If you make more deposits than withdrawals, your account will be large enough to get you through difficulties and back to a joyful life.

Surviving is not enough. Whatever your work, social status, or income level, the resilient life is one of inner peace and security. This doesn't mean that there is no hard work, trouble or chaos. It means to be in the midst of all those things and still be able to bounce back to a fulfilling life every time.

Money and social status don't create resilience. If they did, all the rich and famous would lead happy lives. Your ability to bounce back is primarily internal and achievable by all.

Focusing internally is difficult for both people and companies. We like to keep things impersonal and "professional." We talk about the external things, processes, structures, finances, and economy. Then when things don't seem to be going well we look for someone or something to blame.

Resilient people create resilient families, neighborhoods, companies, and countries. Begin with yourself.

In the next section you can review each of the 52 statements on the BBQ and learn the impact and importance of each one. A "To Do" is provided plus space for notes and your personal action item to increase your bounce backability.

Don't overwhelm yourself by trying to rush through all 52 quickly. Small firm steps are the best. Give yourself time to adjust to a new way of thinking and acting.

"As long as a man's inner nature remains inwardly stronger and richer than anything fate brings his way, good fortune will not desert him. For the superior man everything furthers — even descent."
– The I Ching

(That goes for women, too!)

1
••••••

I use words like choice, can, and will rather than can't, try and maybe.

1	2	3	4	5
Little or none	Some extent	Moderate extent	Great extent	Very great extent

The words you use are indicative of your state of mind and truly create your reality. Even when joking, you betray your inner feelings with word choices. Listen to yourself. If your score was low in this area, ask yourself why you use these negative, restrictive or self-defeating words. It may be habit, a carryover from language you heard growing up. Does it fit with who you are today? Does it fit with who you want to be?

To do: Watch your language, well, at least listen to it. The two most difficult words to eliminate are can't and try. Replace can't with something less final. How about, difficult or complicated? Try, means you might not succeed. Assume success, not failure. Use will instead of try. Consciously change your language. It takes at least two weeks to break a habit and two more to make a new one. If you make it through one month you are well on your way to new language and a new way of thinking and doing.

Notes: _____

_____

_____

_____

_____

_____

_____

Action item: _____

_____

_____

_____

_____

2
·····

I look for ways to keep growing personally and professionally.

1	2	3	4	5
Little or none	Some extent	Moderate extent	Great extent	Very great extent

Still water becomes stagnate. If you find moss growing on your life and career, get busy doing something about it. If you're not sure about the moss, here's a test. What have you achieved during the past year? What have you done to improve yourself? If the list is really short, you may have dry rot! Get off the couch!

To do: Make a list of the things you need to do to keep growing in your life and career. These might include reading books or professional magazines, joining a professional group, taking a class, finding a mentor, attending a seminar, or reevaluating your direction. Each day make a note of at least one thing you have done to keep growing. Small steps add up to giant leaps. It may mean the difference between success and failure in the future.

Notes: _____
_____
_____
_____
_____
_____
_____

Action item: _____
_____
_____
_____
_____

3

I see negative events as a temporary setback, which I can get through.

1	2	3	4	5
Little or none	Some extent	Moderate extent	Great extent	Very great extent

Getting stuck in traffic, losing a job, becoming ill, or having your house blown away by a tornado are all negative events. No one expects you to be happy about them. The question is, to what extent and for how long will they have a negative impact on your life? If you believe you can get through them, you won't get stuck in "victim mentality." Instead, you will take control of what you can and move forward.

To do: Stuck in traffic? Don't let your blood pressure soar. Listen to pleasant music, do some deep breathing or think about something wonderful you've planned. Lost your job? Update your resume, get busy networking, attend professional association meetings. If you find yourself really stuck, catastrophize. Ask yourself, "how could this be worse?" List all the ways. It will help you gain perspective.

Notes: _____

_____

_____

_____

_____

_____

_____

Action item: _____

_____

_____

_____

_____

_____

4
......

I believe it is my responsibility to continue my education or skill building.

1	2	3	4	5
Little or none	Some extent	Moderate extent	Great extent	Very great extent

Lifelong learning is a necessity in today's world. If you scored low here, ask yourself, if not you, whom do you believe is responsible for your education? Your parents? Your company? Who? It is your career and life that will benefit. Go after what you need. If you have a tuition reimbursement program at work, use it. It's a gift. If not, there are scholarships, grants, and financial assistance or you can pay for it yourself.

To do: Make a list of the skills and competencies you will need to succeed in the future. If you're unsure, ask for guidance from your boss, teacher, or mentor. Pay close attention to the career market and where it's heading. Stay ahead of the curve and you won't be left behind. Keep learning.

Notes: _____

_____
_____
_____
_____
_____
_____
_____

Action item: _____

_____
_____
_____
_____
_____
_____
_____

5
......

I surround myself with people who support and encourage me.

1	2	3	4	5
Little or none	Some extent	Moderate extent	Great extent	Very great extent

It is true that you can tell a great deal about people by the company they keep. Your friends and associates reflect what you think of yourself. If you believe you deserve to achieve your personal and professional goals you will surround yourself with supportive people. They will energize and empower you. If you scored low here, ask yourself why?

To do: Make a list of the people who are supportive of your goals. Value them. Whom would you like to add to the list? Why? If you have no supporters, start building your team today.

Notes: _____

_____

_____

_____

_____

_____

_____

_____

Action item: _____

_____

_____

_____

_____

_____

_____

6
......

When an unexpected change occurs, I view it as an opportunity to experience something new.

1	2	3	4	5
Little or none	Some extent	Moderate extent	Great extent	Very great extent

Unexpected change ranges from frustrating to frightening. Fear can paralyze your thinking and keep you from seeing new opportunities and possibilities. If your score was low, begin to look past the fear and let change become a catalyst to energize you and boost your creative thinking into high gear.

To do: When an unexpected change occurs, make three lists.

1) Negative results 2) Positive results 3) New opportunities. Evaluate how the change will impact you. Then, take action to position yourself to take advantage of the new opportunities.

Notes: _____

_____
_____
_____
_____
_____
_____
_____

Action item: _____

_____
_____
_____
_____
_____

7
●●●●●

I ask for advice or help when dealing with a difficult situation.

1	2	3	4	5
Little or none	Some extent	Moderate extent	Great extent	Very great extent

People with low scores will tend to withdraw and feel alone in difficult situations. This is a time to reach out and ask for what you need. Most people are willing to help or advise you if you are clear and reasonable about requests. Others may have more experience or knowledge. Allow them to share it. What do you need? Is it information, resources, advice, or someone to listen?

To do: When you are faced with a difficult situation or decision, make a list of the people who may be able to guide or support you and how they might help. Call them.

Notes: _____

_____

_____

_____

_____

_____

_____

_____

_____

Action item: _____

_____

_____

_____

_____

_____

8

I am willing to take reasonable risks when I recognize a new opportunity.

1	2	3	4	5
Little or none	Some extent	Moderate extent	Great extent	Very great extent

Living requires risk. Whether it's going back to school, asking for a promotion, or venturing into a new career or business. Even if you fail, you'll know that you tried. If you never try, you'll deal with "if only" thinking, maybe for the rest of your life. If you scored low here, ask yourself why you avoid risk taking. Fear of failure and low self esteem are the two strongest barriers. Don't make excuses and defeat yourself before you start. Windows of opportunity don't stay open forever.

To do: What small risk would help you move forward in your life or career? When will you do it?" The first step is always the most difficult. Make the phone call, write the letter, get the book, ask for the raise, but take the necessary risk for your future.

Notes: _____

_____

_____

_____

_____

_____

_____

_____

Action item: _____

_____

_____

_____

_____

_____

_____

9
·····

When my life or work isn't going in the direction I want, I take responsibility and get busy making a plan for change.

1	2	3	4	5
Little or none	Some extent	Moderate extent	Great extent	Very great extent

It's easy to blame a person, a company, or an organization for your problems. If you scored low here, that may be your mindset. When you blame others, you give away your power. When you take responsibility, you empower yourself. Although it may be difficult to face at times, most of what happens in your career and life is up to you. Make a plan.

To do: If you scored low on this question, make a list of everyone or everything you blame for some problem in your life. Look over the list. Ask yourself, "Am I going to let this list continue to have power over my life or am I going to take my power back?" If you want it back, decide what positive steps you can take to redirect your life.

Notes: _____

_____

_____

_____

_____

_____

_____

_____

Action item: _____

_____

_____

_____

_____

10

I have confidence that I can learn to do almost anything if I work at it.

1	2	3	4	5
Little or none	Some extent	Moderate extent	Great extent	Very great extent

New, unfamiliar tasks may be intimidating, especially with cutting edge technology. If your score is low, you may procrastinate, dig in your heels or throw up your hands and say, "I can't." Can't people don't bounce.

Question what you believe about your ability. Limiting beliefs often come from childhood and can be reinforced through the years by others. The word confidence comes from the Latin, with faith, or fidelity. Have faith in yourself. Assume you can. Get training, work hard and achieve.

To do: List your limiting beliefs. Where did you get them? Are they true now? What steps can you take to overcome them? Get rid of old misinformation about yourself.

Notes: _____

_____

_____

_____

_____

_____

_____

_____

Action item: _____

_____

_____

_____

_____

_____

_____

11

When dealing with a new way of doing things, I persist until I'm successful.

1	2	3	4	5
Little or none	Some extent	Moderate extent	Great extent	Very great extent

If your score is low, is it because you resist doing things a new way? Often this is the case. Old methods are familiar and new ones may seem cumbersome or inefficient at first. If you needed to learn to write with your non-dominant hand, you could do it, with time and practice. Persistence is the key.

To do: When a new way of doing things is required, accept this process. 1) Learning 2) Mistakes and frustration 3) Gaining experience 4) More mistakes and frustrations 5) Mastery. Don't give up at steps two and four.

Notes: _____
_____
_____
_____
_____
_____
_____

Action item: _____
_____
_____
_____
_____
_____
_____

12

When I have a setback or failure, I look for the lesson and move on.

1	2	3	4	5
Little or none	Some extent	Moderate extent	Great extent	Very great extent

Failure is not an ending. It's the middle of a process to get you to the goal you're seeking. If your score was low, you may be prone to give up easily. Instead, learn from the failure and make appropriate adjustments to your next steps. Never give up. Success may be just around the corner. The only true failure is a failure to learn.

To do: Anytime you feel you've failed, make three lists. The things you have learned: 1) not to do 2) should have done 3) and will do next time. Creating the lists will keep you from repeating mistakes, help you see the total picture, and guide you to better choices next time.

Notes: _____

_____

_____

_____

_____

_____

_____

_____

Action item: _____

_____

_____

_____

_____

13

I congratulate myself for accomplishments and appreciate the work I've done.

1	2	3	4	5
Little or none	Some extent	Moderate extent	Great extent	Very great extent

Celebrate your successes, even the small ones. Don't say, "It's not that big a deal or it was just luck." Take credit. You deserve it. Every success is self validating. By acknowledging your accomplishments, you strengthen your self image. If your score was low, ask yourself why? Are you lacking accomplishments or do you fail to value yourself?

To do: Give yourself a gift to celebrate. A flower, a decadent dessert, a massage, tickets to a sporting event, or some time just for yourself. Make it proportionate to the accomplishment. Celebrating with friends is great, too. What do you need to celebrate now?

Notes: _____

_____
_____
_____
_____
_____
_____
_____
_____

Action item: _____

_____
_____
_____
_____

14

I don't procrastinate when I have an important task to do.

1	2	3	4	5
Little or none	Some extent	Moderate extent	Great extent	Very great extent

Procrastination is a success destroyer. If you scored low, is it because you don't know what to do, don't know how to do it, don't want to do it, you fail to focus, or you're afraid you will either fail or succeed? What are the consequences of each? Once you can answer those questions you will know how to proceed.

To do: Each morning, ask yourself, "What are the three most important things I need to do today?" Post them on your computer, write them at the top of your to do list, but don't make excuses for not doing them. If you need advice or help, get it. Create a block of time when you don't answer the phone, won't accept interruptions, and can focus on your goal. Think how good you will feel when you have completed your tasks.

Notes: _____

_____

_____

_____

_____

_____

_____

Action item: _____

_____

_____

_____

_____

15

I believe I have an inner or higher source of strength to call on when everything seems to be going wrong.

1	2	3	4	5
Little or none	Some extent	Moderate extent	Great extent	Very great extent

Feeling alone and powerless keeps us from bouncing back in life. When you feel supported by an inner strength or a power greater than yourself, you never feel completely alone. There is a sense of sharing the burden or having it carried for you until you regain your footing. Faith will reinforce your power and allow you to continue in the most difficult times.

To do: Search your beliefs. What is at your core? What power or strength is present that will guide or support you through difficulties? Tap into that power, according to your beliefs, and allow it to support you in bouncing back.

Notes: _____

_____

_____

_____

_____

_____

_____

_____

Action item: _____

_____

_____

_____

_____

_____

16

I watch less than two hours of TV daily.

1	2	3	4	5
Little or none	Some extent	Moderate extent	Great extent	Very great extent

Many wonderful, informative and entertaining TV programs exist. Ask yourself, though, "am I avoiding something more important and valuable to me?" Watching just one hour each day adds up to 15.2 days of your life each year. Two hours daily is a full month annually. Do you ever complain that you don't have enough time? How are you spending yours?

To do: Decide to limit your TV viewing to specific programs and don't waver. Make a list of the programs you currently watch. Mark out all but your favorites. If you have a long list of favorites rethink your priorities. Mindless viewing may temporarily reduce the stress of an important task but ultimately leaves you with less accomplished in your life. Avoid eating while watching TV. It increases your waistline and decreases your willpower to hit the off button.

Notes: _____

_____

_____

_____

_____

_____

_____

_____

Action item: _____

_____

_____

_____

17

I sleep or nap 10 hours or less within a 24 hour period.

1	2	3	4	5
Little or none	Some extent	Moderate extent	Great extent	Very great extent

If you are sleeping more than 10 hours in 24 on a regular basis, see your healthcare professional for a checkup to eliminate any possible illness. Excessive sleep may also be a sign of depression, or a means of avoidance.

To do: Research has shown that regular sleep patterns make for the best rest. Try to go to bed and arise at a regular time each day, including weekends. Too much sleep can actually make you feel tired. One extra hour each day is seven hours a week. In a year, it's over two weeks!

Notes: _____
_____
_____
_____
_____
_____
_____
_____
_____

Action item: _____
_____
_____
_____
_____

18

I forgive myself and move on, when I feel I've made a wrong choice.

1	2	3	4	5
Little or none	Some extent	Moderate extent	Great extent	Very great extent

All of life is a choice. Sometimes we wish we had chosen more wisely. Rehashing mistakes and beating yourself up are wasted effort and emotionally draining. Rather than, "if only," say, "what now?" Forgive yourself, learn from the mistake, make a new choice, and move on.

To do: Is there anything for which you need to forgive yourself? Is there an "if only" that is haunting you? Hanging onto the past is non-productive. However, if you have hurt or harmed someone, take actions to make restitution and ask for their forgiveness. To forgive yourself, take out a piece of paper and write, "I forgive myself for.....”; then write whatever it is you need to forgive. Fold up the paper, and burn it in a safe place. As it burns, let your guilt evaporate with the smoke.

Notes: _____

_____
_____
_____
_____
_____
_____

Action item: _____

_____
_____
_____

19

I let go of old friends or business acquaintances if they are no longer supportive.

1	2	3	4	5
Little or none	Some extent	Moderate extent	Great extent	Very great extent

Hanging on to old friends or business acquaintances is self defeating if they are negative and non-supportive. People who truly care about you may disagree but they don't belittle or put down your ideas or goals. Don't hold yourself back. Your success may intimidate others or make them jealous. That is their problem. Don't make it yours.

To do: What relationships do you need to let go? List them. Begin making changes. Find new friends who will support and encourage you. Remember that true friends are always there for you.

Notes: _____

_____

_____

_____

_____

_____

_____

_____

_____

Action item: _____

_____

_____

_____

_____

20

I look for new and better ways to accomplish tasks.

1	2	3	4	5
Little or none	Some extent	Moderate extent	Great extent	Very great extent

If you scored low here, you are not using your creative abilities. You can always find a better way. Technology may help, a different process, or maybe an entirely new way of thinking. First, ask yourself, "Is this something that really needs to be done?" Often we continue to repeat tasks, reports, or processes that could be eliminated.

To do: Look for at least two "right" answers when searching for new methods. There is seldom just one way to accomplish a task. Then, select the one that works best. What current tasks could be eliminated or done more effectively?

Notes: _____

_____
_____
_____
_____
_____
_____
_____
_____
_____

Action item: _____

_____
_____
_____
_____

21

When I make a mistake, I take responsibility.

1	2	3	4	5
Little or none	Some extent	Moderate extent	Great extent	Very great extent

Don't blame. If you screwed up, own it. You may feel embarrassed, you could be reprimanded, it might even cost you some money. You'll ultimately get more respect from others and feel better about yourself. Not taking responsibility is a sign of insecurity and a lack of self respect. We all make mistakes. The people who can make a mistake and maintain self respect are the ones who bounce back every time.

To do: If you find yourself tempted to blame, take a deep breath, then ask yourself, "how was I responsible? What choice did I make or not make that caused this situation." Then, make corrections, apologize, or do whatever is necessary to make the situation better.

Notes: _____

_____

_____

_____

_____

_____

_____

_____

_____

_____

Action item: _____

_____

_____

_____

22

I weigh the consequences of my actions when I make a decision.

1	2	3	4	5
Little or none	Some extent	Moderate extent	Great extent	Very great extent

A low score indicates potentially serious problems. An unexamined decision on your part could negatively impact you, your family or your organization. Sometimes the impact is immediate, but often it won't be felt for a long time. Whom or what will be helped, harmed, or changed? Does the end justify the means in this instance? Is it for the greater good? Can you live with it?

To do: If you're facing a difficult decision, make a list of all the negatives and give each a weight from 1 – 10 depending on their impact. Do the same for the positives. Add each score to gain a perspective on the impact.

Notes: _____

_____
_____
_____
_____
_____
_____
_____
_____
_____
_____

Action item: _____

_____
_____
_____

23

My work is compatible with my values.

1	2	3	4	5
Little or none	Some extent	Moderate extent	Great extent	Very great extent

Each of us has a set of values, those things which are most important to us in life. If our work is not compatible with at least some of those values, we suffer from emotional conflict and stress. When additional problems or setbacks are added, bouncing back is difficult. If you scored low here, you are more likely to be less productive and become angry or depressed.

To do: What are your five most important values? List them. Are they being met in your work? If not, is there a way you could more fully meet them? If not, begin searching for more compatible work.

Notes: _____

_____

_____

_____

_____

_____

_____

_____

_____

_____

Action item: _____

_____

_____

_____

_____

24

While I think of others, I value and take care of my needs.

1	2	3	4	5
Little or none	Some extent	Moderate extent	Great extent	Very great extent

Self sacrifice is sometimes necessary, but don't become a doormat. Value yourself and your needs and goals. If you don't take care of yourself you can't really take care of others. Maintain a balanced approach. Others will value you to the extent you value yourself.

To do: List what you can do to more fully take care of your needs. Do you value your time? Can you say, "NO," to requests? Do you value your goals?

Notes: _____

_____
_____
_____
_____
_____
_____
_____
_____
_____
_____

Action item: _____

_____
_____
_____

25

I always read the "handwriting on the wall" and decide what I need to do.

1	2	3	4	5
Little or none	Some extent	Moderate extent	Great extent	Very great extent

People who bounce back quickly don't ignore the "handwriting on the wall." They explore options and prepare for what might occur. Think back, have you ever been blindsided by a change and then realized you had an inkling about it all along? Denying or avoiding is setting yourself up to become immobilized in fear or blaming when the truth becomes apparent. Bouncing back could take a long time. A really long time.

To do: Reading the "handwriting on the wall" isn't enough. Investigate, look for options, prepare, and take action. What "handwriting" have you noticed lately? What will you do about it?

Notes: _____

_____

_____

_____

_____

_____

_____

_____

_____

Action item: _____

_____

_____

_____

26

My actions match my words.

1	2	3	4	5
Little or none	Some extent	Moderate extent	Great extent	Very great extent

Your actions truly speak louder than your words. If there is a disconnect, the words mean little and your integrity and credibility are compromised. A low score indicates a need for serious evaluation of your motives.

To do: Evaluate the reasons you have for the mismatch. Are you lying, attempting to impress, lazy, have good intentions but no follow through, or have you been unaware? Learn the cause and begin taking steps to reclaim your credibility. It will take time, but it's worth it.

Notes: _____
_____
_____
_____
_____
_____
_____
_____
_____

Action item: _____
_____
_____
_____
_____

27

When bad things happen, I mourn the loss, understand that this is life and move on.

1	2	3	4	5
Little or none	Some extent	Moderate extent	Great extent	Very great extent

Life is filled with events that frustrate, enrage, hurt, and devastate. Don't deny your feelings; they're part of the healing and recovery process. Allow yourself to mourn. It may take hours, days, weeks, or many months, with a major loss. Mourning is a process, which means it has a beginning and an end. Eventually, you must move on. Life is also filled with joy, excitement, love, and hope.

To do: In difficult times rely on the assistance and support of friends, or professionals, if necessary. Talking about your situation to appropriate people (not everyone) will help you process and bounce back more quickly.

Has something bad happened to you lately? What are you doing about it?

Notes: _____

_____

_____

_____

_____

_____

_____

Action item: _____

_____

_____

_____

28

I am aware that everything I do is a choice, even not choosing.

1	2	3	4	5
Little or none	Some extent	Moderate extent	Great extent	Very great extent

Awareness is crucial. If your score is low, perhaps you let your life just "happen." Even that is a choice. It's a choice not to choose. Awareness gives you control. Conscious choosing will keep you focused and moving in the direction of your goals. When you encounter problems, you will be able to make appropriate choices for solving them and bounce back quickly.

To do: To increase your awareness, remind yourself when you make a choice.

EX: I choose to eat this fattening desert even though I say I want to lose weight. I choose to go to school at night because it will further my career. Repeat to yourself, awareness brings control. Write it on a Post It note and stick it on your bathroom mirror.

Notes: _____

_____
_____
_____
_____
_____
_____
_____

Action item: _____

_____
_____
_____
_____

29

I do my best even when I don't like a particular job.

1	2	3	4	5
Little or none	Some extent	Moderate extent	Great extent	Very great extent

Take pride in the quality of your work. Doing your best wherever you are will help you get to the next level. Dragging your feet may be a way of showing your displeasure or trying to get even with a boss or co-worker but the end result will be lowering your self-esteem and possibly impacting your career. If your score is low rethink your work ethic and attitude. Consistently good performers bounce back quickly.

To do: Examine your work performance. Do you feel good about it? If not, why not? How about the work you do at home? If your answers are negative, list three things you can do to improve. When will you begin?

Notes: _____

_____

_____

_____

_____

_____

_____

_____

_____

Action item: _____

_____

_____

_____

30

I prioritize and break large tasks into manageable parts.

1	2	3	4	5
Little or none	Some extent	Moderate extent	Great extent	Very great extent

Large tasks often appear overwhelming, causing people to delay beginning, sometimes indefinitely. You can't bounce when you're not moving. If you break jobs into smaller doable tasks with a timeline for each you are more likely to succeed. Delegate, if necessary, get advice, when needed, and get started.

To do: If you are avoiding a large task, ask yourself why. Write the reasons below. Fear or unrealistic expectations can keep you stuck. List three small steps you can take to begin. Write the date you will do them.

Notes: _____

_____
_____
_____
_____
_____
_____
_____
_____
_____

Action item: _____

_____
_____
_____
_____

31

I believe that life is for living and enjoy it all.

1	2	3	4	5
Little or none	Some extent	Moderate extent	Great extent	Very great extent

Everyone prefers to work with, buy from, and live with, people who have a positive perspective. The ability to find the humorous, the exciting and the meaningful in life is the same ability needed to bounce back from the unexpected, the sad, and the disastrous. If your score is low you may be stuck in past hurt or anger.

To do: Every day write at least two good things that happened. Even on the worst of days, there is good. When you begin to look for it, you will find it.

What two good things happened today?

Notes: _____

_____
_____
_____
_____
_____
_____
_____
_____

Action item: _____

_____
_____
_____
_____

32

When offered an opportunity for leadership, I'll accept and learn all I can.

1	2	3	4	5
Little or none	Some extent	Moderate extent	Great extent	Very great extent

Everyone has the ability to become a leader at some level. If leadership is new to you, it can be intimidating. Take advantage of the opportunity to learn and gain experience. Ask for advice from a mentor or friend and do your best. You will grow in knowledge, self-confidence, and bounce backability.

To do: To begin developing your leadership skills, start small. Chair a committee or small event. Then it's on to something bigger. What will you do to begin developing your leadership skills? If you are already in a leadership position, what is your next step to a greater challenge?

Notes: _____

_____

_____

_____

_____

_____

_____

_____

Action item: _____

_____

_____

_____

33

I believe bad hair days, soggy sandwiches, or bad coffee are just a part of life, no big deal.

1	2	3	4	5
Little or none	Some extent	Moderate extent	Great extent	Very great extent

Day-to-day irritations can get you down if you tend to see the negative. "Everything bad happens to me." It's far better to laugh at your bad hair, avoid the bread on a soggy sandwich, (you'll save calories), and coffee isn't that great for you anyway. Save your energy for more important matters like bouncing back from "real" problems.

To do: If you become upset over something minor, ask yourself, "what's going on?" Usually the upset is related to some other stress, disappointment, or concern in your life. Identifying it will allow you to deal with the real problem.

Notes: _____

_____

_____

_____

_____

_____

_____

_____

_____

Action item: _____

_____

_____

_____

_____

34

When a problem arises, I face it and set about finding a solution.

1	2	3	4	5
Little or none	Some extent	Moderate extent	Great extent	Very great extent

A low score indicates avoidance. Why do you avoid or put off solving a problem? Awareness is the key. Avoidance increases stress, reduces productivity, steals sleep, and has a tendency to exaggerate the situations impact. A long delay means a long bounce back period.

To do: To solve a problem more quickly: Write the problem at the top of a sheet of paper. Create two columns, one for what will happen if you do nothing, the other for possible resolutions. Then, get busy on the best resolution.

Notes: _____

_____

_____

_____

_____

_____

_____

_____

_____

_____

Action item: _____

_____

_____

_____

_____

35

I have created a "safe space" or oasis where I feel comfortable and relaxed in life.

1	2	3	4	5
Little or none	Some extent	Moderate extent	Great extent	Very great extent

A place to feel safe and comfortable is important to your well being. For some it's the entire home environment, for others a special room or even a well-worn chair. If your score is low, you are probably stressed and feel you are always "on." You are always filling a role. Whether you're a manager, employee, mother or father, you need time to just be you without other requirements. It's a time to renew yourself.

To do: If you don't have a sanctuary create one. Surround yourself with pictures, flowers, candles, old trophies, mementos or whatever pleases you. My grandmother crocheted an afghan for me years ago. When I wrap myself in it I always feel safe, warm, and loved. What do you want in your space?

Notes: _____

_____

_____

_____

_____

_____

_____

_____

_____

Action item: _____

_____

_____

36

I believe that I am in charge of my life.

1	2	3	4	5
Little or none	Some extent	Moderate extent	Great extent	Very great extent

When you believe you're in charge, you will take charge when problems arise. You can't control every event, but you know your response is within your control. If your score was low, you feel that fate, your company, or other people control your life, to a great extent. They don't, unless you allow it. If you don't take charge, you may bounce around for years feeling battered by the bumps, watching others bouncing back above you.

To do: Ask yourself "What benefits do I receive from the belief that I am not in charge of my life?" Yes, there are benefits. You might have someone to blame, receive sympathy, avoid more education, or not have to work as hard. Once you face the benefit you have a choice. Take control and give up the benefit or stay stuck. Stuck is a sticky place. It's not fun and there's no bounce.

Notes: _____

_____

_____

_____

_____

_____

_____

_____

_____

Action item: _____

_____

_____

37

I always bounce back quickly from any change or difficulty.

1	2	3	4	5
Little or none	Some extent	Moderate extent	Great extent	Very great extent

If you believe you're not resilient your score is low. Your beliefs about yourself are what you make happen. Bounce back can be increased. You add to your self image every day. What are you adding? Not good enough, no control, a victim? Or, getting better all the time, taking control, taking responsibility?

To do: At the end of each day, write five things you did that you feel good about. It can be anything from closing a sale to smiling pleasantly at a surly clerk. At the end of the week you'll have 35 positive additions to your self image. At the end of the year you'll have 12,775!

Notes: _____

_____

_____

_____

_____

_____

_____

_____

_____

Action item: _____

_____

_____

_____

38

I have daily rituals, which provide a sense of stability even in chaotic times.

1	2	3	4	5
Little or none	Some extent	Moderate extent	Great extent	Very great extent

Rituals give us continuity and stability. Weddings, funerals, birthday and retirement parties mark special occasions. Small daily rituals provide a comforting sameness, a soothing touchstone that softens the blows of a changing world.

To do: My daily ritual is a cup of hot tea every afternoon, even when I travel. I carry an immersion unit and tea bags to insure that cozy time. For others it's a long hot bath, silent meditation, reading a favorite book or bagels every morning with a friend. Find what makes you feel warm and wonderful even on difficult days. Remember to care for yourself.

Notes: _____

_____
_____
_____
_____
_____
_____
_____
_____

Action item: _____

_____
_____
_____

39

I believe I have a purpose in life.

1	2	3	4	5
Little or none	Some extent	Moderate extent	Great extent	Very great extent

A sense of purpose or mission provides direction in life. The purpose helps determine your goals. Without that central focus you're like a compass with no needle. If you haven't thought about it, do it now. It will renew you and help you bounce back much faster.

To do: Examine your purpose. Why are you here? What drives you? What do you want to accomplish? Answer these questions, refocus and move in the direction of your purpose.

Notes: _____

_____
_____
_____
_____
_____
_____
_____
_____
_____
_____

Action item: _____

_____
_____
_____

40

I have a mentor who provides direction and support in my work and life.

1	2	3	4	5
Little or none	Some extent	Moderate extent	Great extent	Very great extent

Mentors guide, advise, critique, encourage, and support us to become all we can be. If you have never had a mentor find one. At any stage in life, a mentor can help you bounce back faster and higher.

To do: A mentor must be someone who is successful, someone you respect, and someone who believes in you but will tell you the truth and urge you forward. If you know someone who meets that criteria, ask if they are willing to guide you. Note: Mentors aren't your parent, the responsibility for your career and life is yours.

Notes: _____

_____

_____

_____

_____

_____

_____

_____

_____

Action item: _____

_____

_____

_____

41

I am active in a professional or civic organization.

1	2	3	4	5
Little or none	Some extent	Moderate extent	Great extent	Very great extent

Professional associations and civic organizations are wonderful places to develop a network of friends, learn new skills, and stay current with your field. The greatest benefit comes from active participation. Serve on committees, take a leadership position. The investment in time and energy will pay dividends and help you bounce back from any difficulty.

To do: If you belong to a professional or civic group, how could you become more active? If you don't belong, what group would be both valuable to you and benefit from your participation? Take action within the next 48 hours.

Notes: _____

_____
_____
_____
_____
_____
_____
_____
_____

Action item: _____

_____
_____
_____
_____

42
. . . .

I commit to a goal even if it requires sacrifice on my part.

1	2	3	4	5
Little or none	Some extent	Moderate extent	Great extent	Very great extent

If you take the easy road, commitment only if it's convenient, you'll hear more of a thud than a bounce. Invest time and energy in yourself and your goals. Remember that successful people do the things unsuccessful people don't want to do.

To do: Make a note of your most important goal. List what will be necessary to achieve it. Develop a time line, share your goal with a friend or mentor and enlist their help in keeping you on track. If you do some backsliding, don't beat yourself up, get back on track and do whatever is necessary.

Notes: _____

_____

_____

_____

_____

_____

_____

_____

_____

_____

Action item: _____

_____

_____

43

I delegate when someone else can handle a task.

1	2	3	4	5
Little or none	Some extent	Moderate extent	Great extent	Very great extent

You can't do it all yourself. Delegate. Give direction and guidelines, then let go. Delegating may allow others to gain needed experience, utilize the expertise of someone else, and free you to focus on priorities. In the world of work, bouncing back is a group effort.

To do: What do you need to delegate? To whom? How will it help that person? How will it help you?

Notes: _____

_____
_____
_____
_____
_____
_____
_____
_____
_____
_____
_____

Action item: _____

_____
_____
_____
_____

44

I feel positive about my life and future.

1	2	3	4	5
Little or none	Some extent	Moderate extent	Great extent	Very great extent

Chronically negative people are passive. If your score is low, do you watch as others seem to pass you by? Perhaps your attitude is affecting your altitude. A positive attitude will help you bounce back quickly. Bouncing requires movement though. A positive attitude is like a great toy with no batteries. Energy is required for action. When you believe in yourself and your future, you can accomplish your goals if you go after them.

To do: If you don't feel positive, list the reasons why. After each, list what you can do to move to a more positive outcome.

Notes: _____

_____
_____
_____
_____
_____
_____
_____
_____
_____

Action item: _____

_____
_____
_____
_____

45

I am flexible and adapt easily and quickly to changes and new situations.

1	2	3	4	5
Little or none	Some extent	Moderate extent	Great extent	Very great extent

Skyscrapers are built with flexibility to insure they don't break apart in high winds and ground tremors. To bounce back, people must be flexible, too. If your score is high, be sure it isn't just lip service. Is the adapting only external with significant internal conflict? It's a start, but you need to resolve internal issues. If your score was low, why aren't you flexible and able to adapt?

To do: What changes have you had to adapt to in the past? List both personal and professional changes. What skills, techniques, or thinking helped you to make those changes? Use those resources for current situations and add to them.

Notes: _____

_____

_____

_____

_____

_____

_____

_____

_____

Action item: _____

_____

_____

_____

_____

46
. . . .

I collaborate effectively with other people.

1	2	3	4	5
Little or none	Some extent	Moderate extent	Great extent	Very great extent

Working with other people for mutual benefit isn't new, but in today's global economy, it is crucial. Being a strong team member and developing partnerships is necessary for your career and company.

Transpose those same words to your personal life. Are you a strong team member and good partner? If you scored low in either, your bounce will be erratic. If you scored low in both areas, you can't bounce and will be bitter about the setbacks life brings.

To do: Assess what you are contributing to teams, partnerships, or groups. Evaluate both your personal and professional life. Congratulate yourself for your contributions. If you believe improvements or changes are necessary, list them and get started on at least one, immediately.

Notes: _____

_____

_____

_____

_____

_____

_____

_____

_____

Action item: _____

_____

_____

_____

47

I accept my limitations, value my gifts, and keep growing.

1	2	3	4	5
Little or none	Some extent	Moderate extent	Great extent	Very great extent

Limitations don't have to be liabilities. We all have them. Accept them and value your unique set of skills and abilities. Focus on increasing skills and developing your abilities. Keep growing in learning, understanding, and compassion. Scoring low may mean that you linger too long over your limitations whether they are perceived or real. Are you using them as an excuse? Look for your gifts. Expand them. Add to them.

To do: List five skills, abilities, or personal characteristics you value in yourself. Pat yourself on the back. Now list three ways you'd like to grow this year and how you plan to achieve them.

Notes: _____

_____

_____

_____

_____

_____

_____

_____

_____

_____

Action item: _____

_____

_____

_____

48

I keep putting one foot in front of the other when things are rough.

1	2	3	4	5
Little or none	Some extent	Moderate extent	Great extent	Very great extent

Sometimes barriers seem insurmountable. Don't give up or your bounce will bomb. Your steps might be slow and labored, but keep moving forward. Learn from each step. Eventually, the going gets easier and your goal will be in sight.

To do: If you have a barrier that is stopping you from achieving a goal, ask yourself these questions. Is the barrier really an excuse? Do you truly want to achieve this goal? If so, what steps are you willing to take to over come the barriers?

Notes: _____

_____
_____
_____
_____
_____
_____
_____
_____
_____

Action item: _____

_____
_____
_____
_____

49

I recognize that growth for people and companies requires change.

1	2	3	4	5
Little or none	Some extent	Moderate extent	Great extent	Very great extent

Change involves loss. It could be an idea, a way of doing things, a way of being, a job, a place, or a person. Loss is painful. Honor and value the past, but let go to grow. Your past has made you who you are today. Your ability to change and bounce back will determine who you are tomorrow.

To do: Are you resisting change in any area of your life? If so, why? What will happen if you don't change? What will happen if you do change? What must you give up or lose. Answering these questions will guide you in making choices for your future.

Notes: _____

_____

_____

_____

_____

_____

_____

_____

_____

Action item: _____

_____

_____

_____

_____

50

I realize that new problems require new solutions and I look for them.

1	2	3	4	5
Little or none	Some extent	Moderate extent	Great extent	Very great extent

Why do people and companies try to solve new problems with the same old solutions? Habit. There is a well-worn path in our brains that says this is the way to do it. "What if" thinking, new perspectives, and a willingness to risk bring new solutions. Bouncing higher and faster requires a sense of adventure, the excitement of exploring new paths.

To do: Think of a problem you need to solve. Focus on developing multiple solutions. Explore. Make solutions unusual, play with them, look at them sideways, open your mind. List them all, take a break to cogitate, and then, test them with logic. What will work?

Notes: _____

_____
_____
_____
_____
_____
_____
_____
_____

Action item: _____

_____
_____
_____
_____

51

I develop and maintain mutually beneficial relationships in my work and life.

1	2	3	4	5
Little or none	Some extent	Moderate extent	Great extent	Very great extent

Personal and organizational relationships can provide trust, support, reliability, and financial benefit. Whether it's two companies partnering on a multi-million dollar deal or long time friends who are there when you need them, relationships count.

To do: List the long term (more than two years) relationships you have in your personal life. Professional life. Is there a balance between the two? After each write the last time you were in contact. Relationships must be maintained, they aren't self sustaining. Send a card, make a phone call or plan a lunch. If you don't have at least two in both categories, get started today.

Notes: _____

_____
_____
_____
_____
_____
_____
_____

Action item: _____

_____
_____
_____
_____

52

My sense of humor and ability to laugh and have fun help me deal with problems.

1	2	3	4	5
Little or none	Some extent	Moderate extent	Great extent	Very great extent

Laughter is medicine for the soul. It lightens the heart, unburdens the head, and relieves stress. It cleans out the cobwebs and helps us focus more clearly. Laughter is a sign of health and will put more bounce in your life.

To do: If you're going through a difficult time, go see a funny movie, read a funny book, or just laugh with your friends. You'll feel better and think better. Learn to laugh at yourself and the day-to-day problems and embarrassments of life. If you laugh every day, life will be lighter. What have you done for fun this week? What have you laughed about?

Notes: _____

_____
_____
_____
_____
_____
_____
_____

Action item: _____

_____
_____
_____

New Beginnings

If you have completed all the to dos in this book, congratulations! Your bounce backability is much improved. Be vigilant. Don't allow yourself to slip back into old habits, or old ways of thinking. Review occasionally to be certain you're on track or use the Bounce Back Journal™ to guide and support you through the year.

Every dawn brings an opportunity for a new beginning in your career and personal life. Both are like a flowing stream. There are rocks and rapids, snakes and sticks, decay and birth, but the flow continues. You adjust your course by the choices you make. If one in the past was poor, don't dwell on it. Each choice is a new opportunity to practice resilience.

Use this book to keep you aware. Reinforce your strengths and work to improve your weaknesses. Whatever your past, your age, or station in life, you can learn to bounce back faster, higher, and with greater joy in living than ever before.

"This is your life, live it to the fullest."

About the Author

Linda Nash, president of L. J. Nash and Associates, Inc., is a nationally known consultant, speaker, and author. She offers an in-the-trenches perspective to companies, organizations, and individuals who want to insure optimal success through the chaos of change, transition and beyond.

Nash's extensive work with corporations, government, education, healthcare, and religious groups has provided her with a perspective and depth of experience matched by few.

She is co-author of the book *Surviving in the Jungle* and author of *The Shorter Road to Success* and *Becoming the Real You and Getting Paid for It!*

Nash's education includes a BA in English Literature, MBA in Management, and doctoral work in Psychology. She is an adjunct instructor at Cornell University in New York and Washington University in St. Louis.

For information on Nash's consulting, speaking, or coaching services call 1-800-701-9782 or email Lindaljn@aol.com

Give a Gift of Greater Bounce Backability To Friends and Colleagues

Quantity rates available

The Bounce Back Quotient $12.95

Bounce Back Quotient (Assessment only) $9.00

Other books by Linda Nash

The Shorter Road To Success $10.00
A one-a-day motivational book for all ages

Becoming the Real You and Getting Paid For It! $29.95
(A guidebook to finding what you really want to be when you grow up whether you're 18 or 80.)

Group or Individual Coaching with Linda (call 314-725-9782)

Check here ____ to receive Linda's FREE Ezine.

Your name _____ E-mail _____

Fax orders to 314-725-9939 • Phone 314-725-9782
e-mail Lindaljn@aol.com

Make checks payable to
Prism Publications, PO Box 16873, St. Louis, MO 63105

Missouri residents 5.75% tax + Shipping costs: $2.50 / book

Name _____

Organization _____

Address _____

City _____ State _____ Zip _____

Phone _____ Email _____

☐ Charge my credit card

☐ VISA | Card No. / / / / / / / / / / / / / / / / / /

☐ MasterCard | Exp. date _____ Signature _____